against British troops, civilians and members of the island's Turkish minority as EOKA terrorists stepped up their activities when Archbishop Makarios was kidnapped and forced into exile by a misguided British government.

In the United States, black civil rights activists began to push for the freedoms the Supreme Court had ruled they should have, with an inevitable white backlash which would only worsen as time went by.

There was a fairy-tale wedding in Monaco, a secret marriage between a sex goddess and one of the world's most intellectual writers and a farewell from a boxing legend. Boring it wasn't!

RCA Unleash Elvis Presley On Unsuspecting World

HAVING SPENT AN unprecedented $35,000 buying him out of his contract with the small Memphis-based Sun Records, the people at music giant RCA Records weren't about to let *Heartbreak Hotel,* Elvis Presley's first single for them, merely be released this month.

It - and he - was going to get a full no-expense-spared, looky-here hype to ensure the American public discovered what thousands of folk south of the Mason-Dixon had known for the past two years: a major star had arrived.

Aged 21, Elvis Aaron Presley shot to prominence in June 1954 when Sun released *That's All Right Mama.* His unique version of an R&B song by Arthur 'Big Boy' Crudup mixed black blues and white country music to create a punchy hybrid which southern teenagers made an immediate regional hit. When he hit the road and they caught sight of the ex-trucker's lascivious body language, he was off and running, scoring more local hits and inevitably coming to the attention of the RCA fat cats.

By the end of this month, RCA's investment had been proved one of the best in history. *Heartbreak Hotel* was America's No 1 single (and would become Britain's No 2 hit in May), to be followed by year end by eight more million-sellers, his film debut *Love Me Tender,* and a mix of hysteria and controversy guaranteed that Elvis Presley would become one of the most potent, popular and eternal symbols of a generation which decided it wanted to call its own shots.

Prince Rainier To Marry Grace Kelly

World gossip columnists were caught on the hop today when Prince Rainier III, ruler of the tiny French Riviera principality Monaco, announced his engagement to American movie actress and beauty Grace Kelly. The couple will marry in April.

Daughter of a noted high society family, Grace Kelly shot to stardom in 1951, establishing that she was more than a perfectly beautiful face in the 1952 movie High Noon, and confirmed her acting skills by winning an Oscar in the 1954 Academy Awards for her performance in *The Country Girl* and winning plaudits for *Dial M For Murder* and *Rear Window* in the same year.

JANUARY 28

Nigerians Give Queen Warm Welcome

Although there are increasing signs of division in many parts of the British Commonwealth, especially in Cyprus, Kenya, Malaya and South Africa, there was no shortage of enthusiasm in Nigeria today. Huge cheering crowds packed the capital of Lagos to give Queen Elizabeth and the Duke of Edinburgh the warmest of welcomes as they began their first state visit to the west African country which became a British colony in the 1860s.

The welcome began on the 13 mile drive into Lagos from the airport, when thousands lined the road to catch a glimpse of the motorcade as it sped by, raising clouds of thick red dust. Greeted by Chief Adele, President of the city council, at Lagos, the Queen also accepted a bouquet from a five year old boy.

UK TOP 10 SINGLES

1: **Rock Around The Clock**
- Bill Haley & His Comets
2: **Love Is A Many Splendoured Thing**
- The Four Aces
3: **Rock-A-Beatin' Boogie**
- Bill Haley & His Comets
4: **Sixteen Tons**
- Tennessee Ernie Ford
5: **The Ballad Of Davy Crockett**
- Bill Hayes
6: **Meet Me On The Corner**
- Max Bygraves
7: **Love And Marriage**
- Frank Sinatra
8: **The Ballad Of Davy Crockett**
- Tennessee Ernie Ford
9: **Never Do A Tango With An Eskimo**
- Alma Cogan
10: **When You Lose The One You Love**
- David Whitfield

JANUARY 16

Nasser Is New Egyptian Supremo

Egyptian leader since April 1954, and survivor of an assassination attempt in October that year, Colonel Gamal Abdel Nasser (pictured) today took on all the executive powers and title of President to make him the country's *de facto* dictator.

The 38 year-old supremo first came to national prominence as one of the young army officers who deposed King Farouk in 1952 and forced him into exile. After negotiating his way through the ranks of the new regime, he ousted President Neguib while the former general was visiting Sudan, consigning Neguib to a figurehead presidency while he became Prime Minister.

Increasingly anti-West in his pronouncements and dealings, Nasser has spent the last few years attempting to modernize his country while carrying out an escalating fight with Israel in the disputed Gaza territory which separates the two implacable enemies.

Britain Sends More Troops To Cyprus

Responding to growing tension and terrorist activities which have paralyzed the Mediterranean island of Cyprus for the past year, the British government today stepped up the reinforcement of forces in an attempt to head off the threat of escalating violence between local Greek and Turkish communities.

The move - which sees armed paratroops patrolling the streets of Nicosia and Limassol - was prompted by the recent murder of a Turkish policeman by members of EOKA, the Greek nationalist organization seeking an end to British rule and union with mainland Greece.

Outraged Turkish Cypriots threatened to take five Greek lives for every Turk killed by EOKA, and leaders of their community demanded strong action from the island's governor, Field Marshal Sir John Harding, himself an EOKA assassination target last November when a bomb exploded at a dinner he was due to attend.

A British sweep of the Troodos mountain range resulted in the seizure of a vast haul of EOKA arms, ammunition and explosives, and the arrest of three terrorists. Under the terms of the island-wide state of alert imposed by Sir John, the three face the death penalty for carrying weapons.

Sir John is known to have held secret meetings with Archbishop Makarios, the Greek Cypriot leader. Commentators hold out little hope of agreement as long as Makarios maintains his demands for self-determination.

Britain To Get Nuclear Raid Warning System

A new air raid warning system to help protect people from radioactive fall-out was announced in London today by General Sir Sidney Kirkman, Britain's civil defence chief. Costing £240,000 ($700,000), it will rely on messages from members of the Royal Observer Corps based in observation posts at 15-mile intervals around the country and linked by underground telephone lines. With experts currently advising people to stay indoors if there's a nuclear attack - and predicting that those in the area of a blast could suffer radiation side-effects 'for as much as three months' - the system's priority will be to estimate which way radiation clouds are likely to head, and advise the population most likely to be affected.

According to Sir Sidney, this should enable farmers to move livestock indoors and give people a chance to stock up on foodstuffs!

Anti-US Rioters Burn Jordan Hospital

Arab opposition to US support of Israel, which reached a watershed in November 1955 when President Eisenhower agreed to supply arms to the forces of Israeli Prime Minister David Ben Gurion, hit a new peak today in the Jordanian capital, Amman.

An anti-US protest turned into a riot when marchers invaded the city's American hospital and began a looting and burning spree which left the building a smouldering ruin.

The hospital attack would mark a distinct deterioration in relations between the leading Arab states, the US and other Western nations perceived by the region's nationalist and Islamic leaders as pro-Israeli.

Alabama Erupts As Southern Whites Fight Integration

THE TWO-YEAR BATTLE BETWEEN civil rights activists and diehard white conservatives which has raged since the US Supreme Court ruled the racial segregation of southern schools and colleges unconstitutional, reached a new intensity today when a federal court ruled that the University of Alabama must re-admit Autherine Lucy, its first black student.

Meanwhile, the city of Montgomery has witnessed huge protests against the arrest of 115 blacks, including civil rights leader the Rev Dr Martin Luther King (pictured), on charges of illegally organizing a boycott of local buses.

Controversy over Autherine Lucy began the day she was first admitted as a student and was forced to run a gauntlet of abuse and projectiles, including rocks and eggs. University authorities suspended her, claiming they did so to protect her from 'great bodily harm'.

The court's decision appears to support the civil rights movement's view that the college was merely submitting to mob rule, and it remains to be seen if, and how, it will meet the court order to provide Lucy with 'adequate protection' when she returns.

But it is the two-month old bus boycott which poses the greatest threat to law and order. It began in sympathy with Mrs Rosa Parks, a Montgomery woman who refused to move from the whites-only front section of a bus to the designated black seats at the rear. She was arrested and fined, then jailed when she refused to pay the $14 fine her protest incurred.

No Goose-Step For New German Army

Only too aware that there are still widespread reservations in world political circles over the creation of its new army, the West German government is taking immense care over all aspects of their 6,000-man volunteer Bundeswehr.

One possible echo of the Nazi past was stilled in Bonn today when it was announced that West German soldiers will definitely not march in the distinctive goose-step style so beloved by Adolf Hitler and his generals.

Tomatoes And Tear Gas Greet French PM

A barrage of stones and tomatoes greeted France's new socialist Prime Minister, Guy Mollet, as he arrived in Algeria today for talks with French settlers and Arab nationalist leaders, only five days after he took office. He was forced to find refuge in Government House as tear gas canisters were hurled at his car.

Mollet's rough welcome came from settlers who fear he will make concessions to the revolutionary Arab FLN, the National Liberation Front, who have waged a 15 month guerrilla warfare campaign against French colonial authorities.

Government House was surrounded by a force of 3,000 Republican Guards flown in from Paris. They were needed as the settlers laid siege, chanting 'To the gallows, Mollet!' despite the premier's repeated promises that France would not abandon Algeria.

FEBRUARY 29

Bombs Destroy Settlement Hopes In Cyprus Talks

A FRESH WAVE OF EOKA bombings today apparently shattered any hopes Britain's Colonial Secretary, Alan Lennox-Boyd, may have had of reaching agreement with the Greek Cypriot leader, Archbishop Makarios, even though the day began optimistically with a goodwill message from Makarios to Mufti Mehmed Dana, the chief Turkish Cypriot spokesman.

As bombs exploded all over Cyprus, it was obvious that his gesture was the only one the Archbishop intended to make towards achieving compromise.

Lennox-Boyd had arrived in Nicosia with a draft constitution which would allow the Cypriots self-determination, but insisted that the rival Greek and Turkish communities - both of which seek union with their respective homelands - agree to a power-share arrangement.

The Archbishop responded with a repeat of his demands for self-determination. These include a guarantee of a Greek majority under any new constitution, and a complete and unconditional amnesty for all political offenders. As these include a number of EOKA terrorists charged with murder, arson and bombing offenses, the demands are completely unacceptable to Britain.

The scene is set for a showdown.

British troops in Cyprus

Britain Abolishes Death Penalty

Amid a heated public and media debate which included an opinion poll finding that 49 per cent of citizens still favour the death penalty, British Members of Parliament today voted overwhelmingly to abolish it, even when the victims are police or prison officers.

Among the controversial cases which featured prominently in the arguments which raged through radio, press and TV coverage of the issue were the hanging in July last year of ex-model Ruth Ellis for the murder of her racing driver boyfriend and the 1952 execution of 19 year old Derek Bentley for complicity in the fatal shooting of a policeman by his burglary accomplice Christopher Craig, who escaped with a prison sentence because he was only 16 at the time.

There were also continued doubts about the guilt of Timothy Evans, hanged in 1950 for the murders of his wife and daughter in the London house occupied by John Christie, the mass murderer executed in 1953 for the slaying of three women at the same address.

Evans' protestations of innocence would eventually be heard in 1966 when a High Court judge advised the Home Secretary his conviction was unsafe and the Queen granted him a posthumous pardon.

Macmillan Hikes UK Bank Rate To Halt Inflation

Only two months after succeeding RA (Rab) Butler as Chancellor of the Exchequer, Harold Macmillan today announced an increase in the UK bank rate, a tighter credit squeeze and cuts in bread and milk subsidies - all designed to brake Britain's rate of inflation. Government opponents were quick to point out that the new bank rate - a hefty 5.5 per cent - is the highest since 1931, and that was caused by the onset of the Great Depression. Defending the move, the Chancellor said: 'The nation must pause in its pursuit of a higher living standard. Inflation is obstinate and serious'. Macmillan's initiative was made in the knowledge, not announced until March, that Britain's 1955 balance of payments deficit was a hefty £103 million ($310m).

Khrushchev Lays Into 'Brutal Despot' Stalin

DETAILS OF AN ASTONISHING attack by Soviet leader Nikita Khrushchev (pictured) on the 30-year reign of dictator Josef Stalin made world headlines today as details of his recent six-hour address to the 20th Communist Party Conference were leaked to Western media. In the course of his speech, which was occasionally greeted by shouts from outraged delegates, Khrushchev described Stalin as a paranoid murderer, a coward and a military incompetent whose WWII decisions had led Russia to the edge of disaster.

Although Stalin died almost exactly three years ago and most of his most feared lieutenants have been dismissed or executed, Khrushchev's speech is still considered either foolhardy or extremely courageous, given that the Moscow hall was packed with hundreds of regional party leaders who owed their positions to the patronage of Stalin's regime.

Khrushchev spoke frankly about Stalin's pre-war purges, his plots to kill rivals, critics and those who believed themselves to be his friends. He described Stalin's panic and cowardice during WWII and his use of 'brutal force', 'odious falsifications and criminal violations of legality'.

As illustration of Stalin's paranoia, Khrushchev pointed out that of 139 members of the Central Committee elected to office in 1934, only 30 per cent survived the relentless arrest and execution programme the dictator pursued to eliminate imagined enemies. Stalin personally approved long lists of those destined to be wiped out.

Given his years as a trusted Stalin aide and his personal involvement in the purges which resulted in the deaths of untold thousands of Ukrainians, Kremlinologists shared the scepticism of delegates who interrupted Khrushchev with shouts of 'Why didn't you kill him?'

According to Khrushchev, there was little anyone could do: 'There was a reign of terror. You just had to look at him wrongly and the next day you lost your head'.

There are reports that Khrushchev's speech sparked off violent riots in Stalin's homeland, Georgia. But outside the USSR - except Communist China, whose leaders believe Stalin's methods were correct and Khrushchev is supping with the devil - it is being viewed as a clear message that Stalinism is dead and the West can anticipate a marked improvement in its relations with Khrushchev's Soviet Union.

MARCH 9

Makarios Deported From Cyprus

Arriving at Nicosia airport this morning to catch a flight to the Greek capital, Athens, Greek-Cypriot leader Archbishop Makarios and his secretary, Bishop Kyprianos of Kyrenia, were bundled aboard a plane which flew them into enforced exile on the Seychelles island group in the Indian Ocean.

Amid riots and EOKA terrorist threats of a massive retaliatory bombing campaign, Cyprus Governor Sir John Harding accused the Archbishop of being 'a major obstacle to a return to peaceful conditions' who had 'actively supported terrorism'.

In London, Labour Party leader Hugh Gaitskell described the Makarios deportation as 'an act of folly'. It certainly made an EOKA target of Sir John - on March 25 a sweep of his bedroom uncovered a time bomb beneath his bed. Only a faulty timer had saved the sleeping Governor's life.

MARCH 2

Hussein Fires Jordan Army's British Commander

King Hussein of Jordan, the English educated and Sandhurst Military Academy student, today fired Lieutenant General John Glubb, the British commander of the Jordan-based 35,000-strong Arab Legion, acknowledged as the most efficient fighting force in the Arab world.

Glubb, who had served three Jordanian kings since 1939 and was popularly known as 'Glubb Pasha', was given only two hours to leave Jordan with his family. It is widely believed his downfall was due to recent magazine articles suggesting that it was he, and not the 20 year old king, who ran the country. The truth is that King Hussein has bowed to pressure from factions supporting the Arab nationalist movement led by Egypt.

UK TOP 10 SINGLES

1: It's Almost Tomorrow
- The Dream Weavers
2: Memories Are Made Of This
- Dean Martin
3: Rock And Roll Waltz
- Kay Starr
4: Zambesi
- Lou Busch
5: Only You
- The Hilltoppers
6: Memories Are Made Of This
- Dave King
7: Band Of Gold
- Don Cherry
8: See You Later Alligator
- Bill Haley & His Comets
9: Young And Foolish
- Edmund Hockridge
10: Rock Island Line
- Lonnie Donegan

ARRIVALS

Born this month:

1: Mark Todd, New Zealand equestrian king, Olympic gold medalist 1984, '88 and '92

3: Zbigniew Boniek, Polish football star

10: Larry Myricks, US Olympic long-jumper

11: Willie Banks, US triple-jump ace

12: Steve Harris, rock musician (Iron Maiden)

14: Tessa Sanderson, British athlete, world javelin champion

18: Ingemar Stenmark, Swedish world ski champion (86 World Cup wins, World Champion, Olympic Gold 1980)

20: Phillip Oppenheim, British politician

20: Sonia Lannaman, international athlete

21: Ingrid Kristiansen, Norwegian world record holder at 5,000, 10,000 and marathon

DEPARTURES

Died this month:

4: (Cuthbert) Dale Collins, Australian journalist, novelist

MARCH 21

Ike Supports King's 'Weapon Of Love'

PRESSED BY CIVIL rights leaders for support in their fight for an end to segregation in southern states, President Eisenhower today welcomed the call of the Rev Dr Martin Luther King for activists to use passive resistance and 'the weapon of love' and said it was '...incumbent on all the South to show some progress toward racial integration'.

National and world attention this month has been focused on Montgomery, Alabama where Dr King, the Rev Ralph Abernathy and other black leaders vowed to continue their fight after being convicted of organizing bus boycotts. They, and the 113 others arrested, have responded by leading pilgrimages, silent demonstrations and days of prayer.

Prayer is, according to the Rev Abernathy, one of the movement's most powerful weapons. He has called for people 'to pray to Almighty God and get into the hearts of Montgomery's people so that justice may be done'.

There appears to be little justice, however, in the case of Autherine Lucy, the University of Alabama's first black student, suspended after violent protests marked her first day. The University has responded to a federal court order demanding her reinstatement by expelling her on the grounds that she has made 'outrageous, false and baseless accusations' against college officials in interviews.

MARCH 24

Queen Mother Robbed Of National Win

The Grand National, Britain's classic steeplechase is no stranger to drama. In 1951 there were calls for the race to be banned when only three of the 36 entrants finished amid scenes of carnage, calls repeated in 1954 when four horses were killed. This year the drama did not involve fatalities, but it did kill off the dreams of the racing-mad Queen Elizabeth, The

Queen Mother, of owning a National winner. Her mare *Devon Loch* was leading - apparently comfortably - along the final straight, when she jumped for no reason and performed a bizarre splits. Sliding along the ground with her jockey managing to stay on board, Devon Loch regained her feet, only to be passed by *ESB*, the eventual winner.

France Quits Vietnam, Goes Into Algeria

A busy month for French military commanders, March saw one painful chapter end and a new, equally-catastrophic one begin.

On March 26, the last French troops left the South Vietnamese capital, Saigon. Their attempts to support the rule of the now-deposed Emperor Bao Dai and defeat the North Vietnamese communist Viet Minh guerrilla army of Ho Chi Minh, ended disastrously in 1954 with the massacre of French forces defending positions at Dien Bien Phu.

But it was trouble nearer home which concentrated French minds. While their government conceded victory to Tunisian and Moroccan nationalists by granting both North African countries their independence, they were determined to retain control of Algeria.

On March 18 a massive airlift began landing thousands of crack troops, arms and supplies in Algeria.

MARCH 15

Broadway Bows To Fair Lady Julie

Broadway gained a new star and the hottest ticket in New York tonight when English singer Julie Andrews' (pictured) performance on the opening of the musical *My Fair Lady* had theatre critics searching for fresh superlatives.
 In fact, everything about the show seems to have won their notoriously-cold hearts - the elegant playing of co-star Rex Harrison, the songs of Lerner and Loewe, and the lush staging.
 Based on George Bernard Shaw's play *Pygmalion*, the show gave 21 year old Julie - a star in Britain since her early teens, and a royal family favourite - the chance to use the role of Eliza Doolittle, the cockney flower seller transformed into a well-spoken society beauty by Rex Harrison's Professor Henry Higgins, as her passport to American and international stardom.
 You could say she succeeded.

OSCARS GO TO FLUFFY FLICKS, QUALITY OVERLOOKED

The Academy of Motion Pictures Arts and Sciences is a body which has, through the years, shown an outstanding ability to overlook films and performances which deserved at least a nomination for their directors and players even if - in their infinite wisdom - the voting members decided to award the Oscars to someone else. This year was an outstanding example to prove the point.

Consider this: eligible for consideration in the 1956 Oscars were John Ford's *The Searchers,* Nicholas Ray's *Invasion Of The Body Snatchers* and *Bigger Than Life,* Kirk Douglas' powerful and effective portrayal of Vincent Van Gogh in *Lust For Life,* and Alfred Hitchcock's *The Wrong Man.*

Result? Only one of those (Douglas) was even nominated, and it's widely recognized that some of those who did win did so with films or performances which were either insubstantial fluff, or by far the least good of careers otherwise full of excellence.

In competition against *Giant, The King And I, Friendly Persuasion* and *The Ten Commandments,* Mike Todd's *Around The World In Eighty Days* was awarded the Best Picture prize. If it was the best movie of the year, how come none of the cast was even nominated for an acting Oscar? Cynics suggest Todd's incredible overspend had to be recouped somehow, and an Academy Award-tagged re-release could maybe do that.

The Director's award went to George Stevens for *Giant,* and while both the recently-dead James Dean and the fast-improving Rock Hudson were nominated as Best Actor for that film, the Academy decided it should go to Yul Brynner for his impression of a wooden-faced zombie in *The King And I.* Nominated, but passed over, was Laurence Olivier's astonishing and timeless portrayal of another king (in *Richard III*) and Kirk Douglas' majestic Van Gogh.

With the competition including Carroll Baker's nymphet in *Baby Doll,* Katharine Hepburn in *The Rainmaker,* and Deborah Kerr's film-saving governess in *The King And I,* Ingrid Bergman must have been astonished to win the Best Actress prize for *Anastasia,* one of the least effective performances of a distinguished career.

In a rare show of excellent judgement, the Academy did award the Supporting Actor prize to Anthony Quinn for his robust Gaugin in *Lust For Life,* but that hardly constitutes a saving of faces. Those reddened even further when it was discovered that the 'Robert Rich' they'd decided deserved an Oscar for his screenplay for *The Brave One* was, in fact, Dalton Trumbo, a writer blacklisted after being named as a communist sympathizer in the Un-American Activities hearings, while the Best Original Screenplay award was given to Albert Lamorisse for *The Red Balloon,* a film with no dialogue!

All in all, the 1956 Oscars are probably one night Hollywood would prefer you'd forget to remember.

APRIL

Polish Prisoners Freed In Soviet Thaw

The Soviets today gave the world one of its most positive signs that its de-Stalinization campaign is genuine when the government ordered the immediate release of a number of Polish leaders locked up by the dead dictator.

Among those liberated is Wladyslaw Gomulka, until 1949 the Polish Communist Party Chairman.

He was lucky to avoid the ultimate sanction when he was arrested and charged with supporting the revisionist beliefs of Yugoslavian leader Tito. In his now-famous 'secret' speech to the 20th Party Congress, Khrushchev said that Stalin had ordered the deaths of the entire Polish leadership.

World Tunes In To See Rainier Marry Movie Princess

A WORLD AUDIENCE OF millions was able to have a close-up view of events in the tiny Mediterranean principality of Monaco today when television cameras recorded the fairy-tale wedding of Prince Rainier III, head of the ruling Grimaldi family, and the beautiful Hollywood princess Grace Kelly.

More than 1200 guests attended the Roman Catholic nuptial mass, with dignitaries from 25 nations mingling with family and luminary friends from European and American high society.

Sponsorship of US coverage came, naturally enough, from leading perfume and beauty product companies, with Camay Soap winning the battle to have the ad break nearest to the new princess's whispered 'I do'.

From Small Things...

In Chicago today, the unveiling of a new technology which excites its inventors, but many science commentators believe is a limited-appeal gimmick only specialists are likely to want or use. In brief, its a device which - like an audio tape recorder - can capture, store and play back television programmes. The general view is that the new invention will probably prove beneficial to TV companies as a way of by-passing network reception problems in remote areas. But its appeal to the general public? Limited, is the verdict.

Whites Attack Singer Cole As Buses Liberated

A sinister development today in the segregation war being fought across the Deep South when a gang of white men dragged the popular black entertainer Nat 'King' Cole from the stage during a show in Birmingham, Alabama and beat him up.

Cole, whose highly-rated network TV show has raised the ire of southern conservatives who object to him duetting with white female performers and addressing them in too-friendly terms, suffered extensive cuts and bruising, but was able to leave hospital the next day.

The attack, witnessed by a predominantly white audience of 3,000, has sent shock waves through the US. While it may have given Cole's assailants satisfaction, it only serves to confirm the worst fears of civil rights sympathizers.

Victory in the Montgomery bus dispute came on April 23 when the City Bus Lines company announced it was ending the practice of segregated seating in its fleet.

UK TOP 10 SINGLES

1: The Poor People Of Paris
- Winifred Atwell

2: It's Almost Tomorrow
- The Dream Weavers

3: Rock And Roll Waltz
- Kay Starr

4: Only You
- The Hilltoppers

5: Memories Are Made Of This
- Dave King

6: Zambesi
- Lou Busch

7: Memories Are Made Of This
- Dean Martin

8: See You Later Alligator
- Bill Haley & His Comets

9: Theme From The Threepenny Opera
- Dick Hyman Trio

10 My September Love
- David Whitfield

APRIL 26

Anthony Eden Wins Khrushchev's Vote

IT MAY BE THE LAST ENDORSEMENT he could have anticipated, or wanted, but British Prime Minister Sir Anthony Eden received the strangest compliment of all from Soviet leader Nikita Khrushchev today - he was reported as saying that, if he was British, he'd vote for Eden's Conservative Party!

The remark was admittedly made by Khrushchev after a particularly alcohol-rich dinner during which he'd swapped angry words and insults with the volatile shadow cabinet minister George Brown, another man notoriously-fond of a drop or six and equally liable to speak his booze-fuelled mind. But it reflects the remarkably conciliatory tone the Soviet visitors adopted for their eight-day visit to Britain.

Not that their talks with the UK government produced any breakthrough. Khrushchev and Soviet premier Nikolai Bulganin did not change their stance on European security, but did contribute fully to talks an official communique described as filled with 'a spirit of candour and realism'.

Although that's usually officialspeak for 'blazing rows and rudeness', Khrushchev's pragmatic summing up - 'You do not like communism. We do not like capitalism. There is only one way out - peaceful co-existence' - met with the British team's full approval.

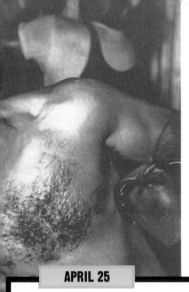

APRIL 17

Churchmen Attack New UK Bond 'Lottery'

The British government's introduction today of a £1 ($3) Premium Bond which gives investors the chance to win up to £1,000 ($3,000) tax-free in a monthly draw, came under attack from leading churchmen who shared the opposition's opinion that the scheme was 'a squalid raffle'. The harshest criticism came from the Archbishop of Canterbury, Dr Michael Ramsey, who said Premium Bonds 'debase the nation's spiritual economy' and were no more than an incitement to gamble.

Introduced by Chancellor of the Exchequer Harold Macmillan, the bonds are part of a government 'Savings Budget' plan to encourage the public to save more, although there will be a £250 ($750) limit on individual holdings. The Chancellor also announced tax relief on annuity payments made on some pension schemes.

APRIL 25

Unbeaten Marciano Calls It A Day

A remarkable chapter in the history of world boxing ended today when Rocky Marciano - never beaten as a professional and undisputed world heavyweight champ since 1952 - announced his retirement at the age of 33 from the sport he'd dominated all his adult life.

Born Rocco Marchegiano, the eldest of six children of a Brockton, Massachusetts immigrant shoe-maker, he was originally rejected by the famous New York matchmaker Al Weill. Only 5'11", Marciano was considered too short to make it as a heavyweight.

Weill changed his tune when Marciano won his first 35 professional fights in just 146 rounds, and the ascendancy of this uncompromisingly-brutal (in the ring) fighter began. Victory over former champion Joe Louis led to a title fight with 'Jersey' Joe Walcott which Marciano won after Walcott had knocked him down in the opening round.

During the next two and a half years, Marciano defended his title six times, with Ezzard Charles the only one able to take him the distance. Marciano's last victory - a ninth round k.o. of Archie Moore in September last year - left him with a carefully-managed $4 million (£1.3m) fortune and a desire to spend more time with his family.

Self-Service Stores Still Stymie Shopper

Although it's more than eight years since the first self-service grocery store opened for business in Britain, it's a concept a large number of UK women are finding easy to resist.

Attempting to explain self-service and dispel old-wives tales of confusion, chaos and (shock horror) multiple choice, the J. Sainsbury grocery store chain took the unprecedented step this month of launching a newspaper ad campaign in the areas where it's switched to the 'new' method.

A step-by-step guide of the process, including instructions on how to use the free trolleys, the company hope the ads will encourage Mrs Britain to use stores which, despite the reservations of many, have resulted in hugely-increased sales.

Opponents of self-service warn that converts will be 'lured into over-spending' and tempted to pilfer. The new stores remove the personal touch of smaller shops, which face closure because of their inability to compete with big-store prices.

MAY 1

Germans March For Unification

Berlin, the pre-war capital of Germany now stranded behind the border which separates West Germany from the communist-controlled East German Republic, is the natural

focal point of most demonstrations by those in the west who seek reunification of the two nations.

Its symbolic importance was dramatically

reinforced today when 100,000 people - young and old - marched through the streets of West Berlin to publicize their desire for the rival governments to bury their differences.

MAY 18

Algerians Massacre French Soldiers And Settlers

THE ALREADY-BLOODY ALGERIAN conflict reached a new horrific level today when a search party sent to find a 19-man French army patrol missing in mountains between Constantine and the capital, Algiers, found their bodies in a silo near a nomad camp. They had been hacked to death and decapitated.

It is only the latest and most gruesome atrocity in a war which has witnessed an escalation of savagery by both sides - the French troops now charged with eliminating pro-independence nationalists, and the Arab FLN guerrillas determined to end French rule.

A week ago, FLN terrorists murdered 20 settlers and burned farmsteads near the city of Oran, while a total of 16 more French soldiers have been killed in action in the Tlemcen region near the Moroccan border. A further 20 have been taken prisoner.

Support for the FLN appears to be growing. Although they could only boast a force of a few hundred when their insurrection began in 1954, French intelligence chiefs now admit the FLN have thousands of recruits.

They no longer scorn a movement which has killed more than 1,000 pro-French Arabs and in excess of 100 European civilians.

MAY 9

Angry Porter's Kitchen Sink Drama

Jimmy Porter is young. He's angry - at his middle-class wife, at his job, at his prospects, at the government. At life in general, if truth be told. He's also the central character in Look Back In Anger, a powerful and controversial anti-establishment tirade of a play by new British writer John Osborne which opened at London's Royal Court Theatre tonight.
 Produced by the English Stage Company and starring Kenneth Haigh as Osborne's disenchanted hero, Look Back In Anger opened the floodgates on a torrent of gritty and powerful so-called 'kitchen sink' dramas by young playwrights prepared to tackle contemporary issues in an uncompromising way. Jimmy Porter, of course, wasn't every critic's cup of tea. One described him as 'a young pup', another as being 'rotten with self-pity'. Kenneth Tynan stuck his neck out, proclaiming Osborne had written 'the best young play of its decade' and Jimmy Porter represented the modern generation 'as it really is'.

MAY 14

UK Admit Spy Link In 'Lost Frogman' Puzzle

THE BRITISH GOVERNMENT today admitted that Commander Lionel 'Buster' Crabb (pictured)- the naval frogman who disappeared in Portsmouth Harbour while the Soviet cruiser which carried Russian leaders Nikolai Bulganin and Nikita Khrushchev to Britain was moored there - had been carrying out trials of 'certain equipment'.

Typically, the government remained coy about the actual nature of that equipment, but it's widely assumed that Crabb and other personnel had been sent out to fix top-secret listening devices to the hulls of the Soviet cruiser Ordzhonikdze and its two escort destroyers when he vanished. It's an assumption the Russians have been quick to use as an excuse to have the Communist Party newspaper Pravda bluster accusations of 'dirty work by enemies of international co-operation' and describe the episode as 'shameful underwater espionage'.

Crabb's disappearance continues to fascinate conspiracy theorists. Although his body would be found - in the waters of Chichester Harbour, some 15 miles east of Portsmouth, in June 1957 - to end speculation that he'd been captured by the Russian Navy, it was headless.

MAY 7

Health Minister Rejects Anti-Smoking Ads

Despite a growing body of independently-researched evidence on both sides of the Atlantic that smoking cigarettes may do more than make you look really cool and transform you into the most irresistibly attractive person in the room, British health lobbyists had a severe knock-back today when the government turned down their requests for a nationwide anti-smoking campaign. Announcing his decision, Health Minister Mr R Turton said he was not convinced that smoking causes any harm. He may be speaking the truth, but cynics have been quick to point out that a reduction in smoking would lead to an inevitable drop in the millions the government receives annually from tobacco-related taxes.

Cyprus Authorities Put A Price On EOKA Leader's Head

The British authorities in Cyprus have put a price on the head of Colonel George Grivas, the EOKA terrorist commander who has so far escaped an island-wide manhunt.

Posters appeared everywhere today, offering a £10,000 ($33,000) reward for information leading to his capture and promising informants protective custody and free passage to 'anywhere in the world'.

A fierce and committed nationalist, Colonel Grivas gained notoriety for his brutal treatment of communist prisoners during the Greek civil war and was a noted leader of resistance forces during the Nazi Germany occupation of Greece during WWII.

The man who signs his orders 'Dighenis' - literally, 'two peoples' - has repeatedly sworn that EOKA's sole target is enosis, the union of Cyprus with Greece.

The urgency for Grivas' arrest was reinforced on May 21 when one person was killed and another 12 hurt in renewed clashes in Nicosia.

JUNE

British Troops Leave Suez Zone

In a simple ceremony held at 6.30 this morning, a British brigadier offered his hand to an Egyptian colonel, saluted and walked up the gangway of a transport ship headed for Cyprus. The British army had left the Suez Canal Zone. Their departure came five days ahead of the deadline set in the 1954 agreement Egypt and the UK signed to end more than 100 years of British presence in the region. Civilian technicians are to remain on the last British base to help Egyptians with maintenance.

UK: Death Penalty Not Dead

Anti-hanging campaigners, who thought they'd won the battle to end capital punishment in Britain, suffered a major setback in the House of Commons today when members voted to retain hanging for murders committed by prisoners already serving life sentences.

In February, MPs had voted for abolition at a first reading of the Bill, but subsequent amendments designed to give prison staff greater protection caused many to re-think their position.

Two other amendments - to retain the death penalty for killing a police officer, and in the course of armed robbery - were defeated. The Bill still has to undergo debate in the House of Lords, and no-one's betting against one of the upper house introducing even more amendments to muddy the once-clear waters.

Monroe Marries Miller

ASTONISHING EVERYONE EXCEPT FRIENDS who knew they really were ascloseasthis, screen sex goddess Marilyn Monroe and intellectual playwright Arthur Miller ended months of gossip column speculation today when they married secretly in White Plains, New York.

It certainly seemed an unlikely match. Arthur Miller, via provocative and intelligent plays such as *All My Sons, View From The Bridge* and *Death Of A Salesman*, was established as one of America's most exceptional and controversial writers - reputations enhanced when he was hauled before the witch-hunting Senate Un-American Activities Committee earlier this month and refused to name names. Ruled to be in contempt of Congress next year, Miller would spend two years winning an appeal and use the experience to write *The Crucible,* his masterpiece about the 17th century Salem witch trials.

Monroe, while not the airhead of popular image, was a pretty mixed-up kid. Emotionally fragile, wracked with terror and anxiety about acting, she was notoriously promiscuous and prone to submerge her fears in cocktails of drugs.

The two first met in New York, when Monroe was filming *The Seven Year Itch* and still tempestuously married to baseball legend Joe DiMaggio. Instant attraction led to an affair, Miller's divorce from his wife of 15 years, Monroe's overnight conversion to Judaism and the secret wedding days before Monroe left for London to begin filming *The Prince And The Showgirl* with Sir Laurence Olivier.

The uncharitable compared their union to a match between Betty Boop and Einstein and predicted a brief, stormy and unhappy relationship. While it was often the latter two, their marriage would actually survive until September 1960 when, thanks mainly to her non-too-private affair with French actor Yves Montand and her increasingly wayward behaviour during location filming of Miller's *The Misfits,* the inevitable happened.

TOP 10 SINGLES

1: I'll Be Home
- Pat Boone
2: Lost John/Stewball
- Lonnie Donegan
3: No Other Love
- Ronnie Hilton
4: Heartbreak Hotel
- Elvis Presley
5: A Tear Fell
- Teresa Brewer
6: Hot Diggity
- Perry Como
7: The Saints Rock 'n Roll
- Bill Haley & His Comets
8: My September Love
- David Whitfield
9: Blue Suede Shoes
- Elvis Presley
10: Too Young To Go Steady
- Nat 'King' Cole

Born this month:

5: Richard Butler, rock singer-songwriter (Psychedelic Furs)
6: Björn Borg, Swedish tennis superstar
8: Russell Christian, singer-saxophonist (The Christians)
9: Berit Aunli, Norwegian Nordic Skiing champion
11: Joe Montana, all-time great quarterback (Notre Dame, San Francisco 49ers, Kansas City Chiefs, Super Bowl MVP 1982, '85, '90, eight Pro Bowls, six-time All-Pro; Tony Allcock, UK and World Bowls Champion
12: Terry Alderman, Australian Test cricketer
26: Chris Isaak, US rock singer

DEPARTURES

Died this month:

11: Sir Frank Brangwyn, British painter

JUNE 25

Senator Kennedy Announces Democrat Nomination Bid

John F Kennedy, the 38 year old Massachusetts senator who entered Congress in 1952 with a shock victory over Republican elder statesman Henry Cabot Lodge, proved himself to be no shrinking violet today when he announced his intention of becoming the Democratic Party's vice-presidential candidate in this year's election.

The young senator, son of Boston millionaire Joseph Kennedy, is a Harvard graduate and former US Navy gunboat commander. While his rise has been meteoric, it is obvious much of his support is due to his father's influence, although he has proved himself an energetic and able constituency politician.

With the Democrats certain to choose Adlai Stevenson as their presidential candidate, commentators believe the party's kingmakers will consider Kennedy too inexperienced to act as his running-mate. It is also felt that Kennedy's Roman Catholic faith is likely to block his chance of major public office now, or in the future.

JUNE 1

Molotov Steps Down As Soviet Man Abroad

Vyacheslav Molotov, one of the last hardline survivors of the Stalin era, was ousted by Nikita Khrushchev today, when it was announced that he had resigned as the USSR's Foreign Secretary - a post he'd held since 1939. His successor is Dmitri Shepilov.

Nicknamed 'stone arse' by Stalin because of his ability to sit unmoving through endless hours of Party Congress sessions, Molotov's slavish loyalty to the dictator was such that he didn't protest when his Jewish wife was sent to the gulag. Appointed Secretary of the Central Committee by Lenin in 1921, he was Prime Minister of Russia from 1930 to 1941 and helped Stalin create the post-war eastern bloc at the Yalta Conference. Now aged 65, his place in the spotlight is over.

JUNE 19

Big-Mouth Pirie Smashes 5,000-Metre Record

Five years ago, London-based athlete Gordon Pirie (pictured) raised titters and red faces when he announced he intended one day to run 5,000 metres in less than 13 minutes 40 seconds.

The titters came because, at that time, the world record stood at 15:58.2. The red faces belonged to British athletics nabobs - dash it all, Englishmen don't boast like that, it's just not on!

Today, the tall rangy star of the South London Harriers Club proved his prediction when, on the Bergen track in Norway, he beat European champion and arch rival Vladimir Kuts and set a new world record time of 13 minutes 36.8 seconds.

38 Killed As Polish Workers Riot Against Communism

MARTIAL LAW WAS DECLARED in the Polish city of Poznan today after anti-government riots by workers left 38 people dead - many of them local Communist Party officials murdered by demonstrators enraged when police opened fire on their march.

The riots, led by rail workers and intended to protest a recent hike in bread prices and the Polish government's decision to impose a wage freeze, appear to have begun as a well-humoured march of a few hundred workers shouting 'Higher wages!' and 'Cheaper bread!' slogans.

All that changed when the police opened fire. When protestors heard a child had been shot, they turned into a savage mob which converged on secret police headquarters and the town hall - controlling both buildings until driven out by a force of tanks and machine gun fire. The confrontation took place only streets away from Poznan's Exhibition Hall, site of an international trade fair. Among the delegates who witnessed events was British businessman Bernard Buckman. He confirmed that the switch from peaceful demo to ferocious street-fighting was due entirely to police action and described rioters as 'roaring with rage' as they headed for the secret police HQ.

JUNE

AUSTRALIAN SWIMMERS TRIUMPH IN WAR-SHADOWED MELBOURNE OLYMPICS

The first Olympic Games to be held in the Southern hemisphere, the Melbourne celebration of the Corinthian ideal was held in the shadow of Russia's crushing of the Hungarian revolution only two weeks earlier. Remarkably, especially if you think about the boycotts and pull-outs which would affect future Games, the Hungarians actually fielded a national team, even if some of their stars were understandably absent!

Declared open by the Duke of Edinburgh on November 22 (when it's summertime in Australia, remember), the '56 Games gave the host nation a chance to show the world just how much their swimmers had come to dominate the aquatic arena. They seized the opportunity - and a ton of metalware - with relish.

Australia carried off five gold medals in the men's events, with Jon Hendricks leading a one, two, three clean sweep in the 100m freestyle race and earning a second gold as a member of Australia's victorious 4X200m freestyle squad.

Dawn Fraser, darling of the Aussie women's team, proved her star billing with two of their three gold medal haul - a solo win in the 100m freestyle, the other in the 4X100m relay - and a silver in the 400m freestyle, in which she was pipped by team-mate Lorraine Crapp, silver medallist behind Dawn in the Australian 100m whitewash in which Faith Leech had claimed the bronze.

On land, all eyes were on Russian Vladimir Kuts, the long-distance ace due to meet British rivals Gordon Pirie and Derek Ibbotson in the 5,000m, and - by the greatest irony of all - Hungary's Jozef Kovacs in the 10,000m. In that event, admiration for Kuts the athlete was tempered by deep sympathy for the country Kovacs represented and

loathing of the nation whose colours Kuts wore.

It was Kuts who won. Whether or not he was aware of the hidden agenda, he stormed away in the 5,000 final to beat Pirie by 11 seconds, with Ibbotson taking the bronze a further four seconds behind. His margin of victory in the 10,000 was not as emphatic - Kovacs took silver less than seven seconds adrift - but the scale of his double achievement certainly was. Vladimir Kuts proved he was the best in the world.

Once again, American athletes dominated the sprints, with Rob Morrow taking gold in the men's 100m, the 200m and the 4X100 relay. His US team-mate Thane Baker had taken silver in the 100 (with local boy Hector Hogan winning bronze), but he had to settle for third in the 200 when Andrew Stanfield got between him and Morrow to make it a USA triple medal event.

Local pride was restored in the women's sprints, when Betty Cuthbert became Olympic champion in both the 100m and 200m. Uniquely, both races finished with the same three athletes in the same winning order - Cuthbert (gold), Germany's Christa Stubnick (silver) and Australian Marlène Matthews (bronze).

With Gordon Pirié unsuccessful against Kuts, Britian's hope of a track gold - its first since 1932 - rested on Chris Brasher, who was running in the 3,000m steeplechase. It was a tight race, with the main contenders still bunched together as they entered the last lap. After a spell of bumping and boring, Brasher broke free of the pack and crossed the line first, only yards ahead of Hungarian Sandor Rozsnyoi. Triumph turned to three hours of anxiety while officials considered a complaint that Brasher interfered with another runner during that last-lap jumble. Verdict? Not guilty. Decision? Gold for Brasher and for Britain.

FOOTBALL
OFFICIAL: REAL KINGS OF EUROPE

May 13: Spanish champions Real Madrid stamped their mark on European soccer history for the first time today when they beat Stade de Reims 4-3 in the first-ever European Cup Final at a sold-out Parc des Princes Stadium in Paris, sending out a clear signal that they were the real kings of Europe - and planned to stay so for some time to come.

The tournament itself was a triumph for French sports journalist Gabriel Hanot, a former international full-back who'd overcome initial apathy and, in the case of the English League, stupidity of national associations to create a pool of 16 club sides to compete for this new trophy.

Not all competing clubs were national league champions. Scottish representatives Hibernian had only finished fifth in the previous season. English champions, Chelsea, gave in to a Football League ruling that the tournament would complicate the domestic fixtures and declined the offer to take part.

The 29 knock-out games saw a feast of goals, 127 in all, with Real Madrid and Reims promising a great final by scoring 20 and 18 respectively *en route*. But it was Real's day.

Even though they fell behind to two quick goals, Real

began to take control of the game. Led by the brilliant Alfredo DiStefano, the Argentinian goal machine who'd just joined them, the sides went in 2-2 at half time, thanks to DiStefano and Rial.

Reims came out firing on all cylinders for the second half, regaining the lead in the 63rd minute via Hidalgo. This was too much for Real. Clamping the game down, they began a spell of tight possession which ended in the 72nd minute with a Marquitos shot which beat Reims goalkeeper Jacquet. Rial was on hand to add the finishing touch to a DiStefano-inspired move which put Real in the lead for the first time at the 80 minute mark. It was a lead they would not give up.

For the record, the Real Madrid team were on a £400 ($1,200) a man bonus to win - the biggest ever offered to soccer players at that time.

Vladimir Kuts - proved he was the best in the world

JULY 1

Two Crashed Airliners Found In Grand Canyon

THE WRECKAGE of two airliners - a TWA Super Constellation and a United Airlines DC-7 - which vanished yesterday, were discovered in the Grand Canyon this morning by the pilot of a small aircraft involved in the massive search which followed their disappearance.

Both aircraft had left Los Angeles within minutes of each other, following an initially similar route. The TWA flight, with 64 passengers and six crew, was bound for New York via Kansas City, St. Louis and Washington DC. The United plane was headed for Chicago with 53 passengers and five crew.

Shortly after crossing into Arizona, the TWA captain asked for, and was given, permission to climb 1,000 feet to avoid turbulence. That brought him within 1,000 ft of the United flight's elevation course of 21,000. Both planes then entered what was, at the time, uncontrolled air space, so the alarm was not raised until neither acknowledged calls from their next check points.

All aboard both flights were killed in what a subsequent Civil Aeronautics Board inquiry decided was a collision caused when the pilots 'did not see each other in time, in cloud'. The tragedy led to an expansion and modernization of traffic control systems which the Federal Aviation Authority had in place by 1958 to ensure there were no more uncontrolled areas of US air space.

JULY 10

Lords Vote To Retain Hanging

Another major hiccup in the campaign to abolish hanging in Britain today when the House of Lords voted overwhelmingly to retain capital punishment for all cases of murder.

Abolitionists had hoped that last month's setback in the House of Commons would be modified or eliminated when the upper chamber debated the issue for the second time. In the event, their lordships went for the unconditional option.

There remains a third reading of the Bill to go before all hope is lost. The anti-hanging lobby will have to go all out to change so many apparently-fixed minds before that happens, however.

UK TOP 10 SINGLES

1: I'll Be Home
- Pat Boone

2: Heartbreak Hotel
- Elvis Presley

3: All-Star Hit Parade
- Various Artists

4: Why Do Fools Fall In Love
- Frankie Lymon & The Teenagers

5: I'm Walking Backwards For Christmas/Bluebottle Blues
- The Goons

6: Hot Diggity
- Perry Como

7: Lost John/Stewball
- Lonnie Donegan

8: Experiments With Mice
- Johnny Dankworth

9: The Wayward Wind
- Gogi Grant

10: The Saints Rock 'n Roll
- Bill Haley & His Comets

JULY 27

Test Match Sensation: Laker 19 – Australia 0

A sensational score-line in the fourth Test between England and Australia today when Jim Laker, the Yorkshire-born off-spin bowler who plays for the Surrey county side, took 19 Australian wickets and racked up the best bowling figures ever recorded in a first-class cricket match. Laker's achievement - a stunning nine wickets for 37 runs in Australia's first innings, and a clean-sweep ten wickets for 53 in the second - was all the more remarkable as his rhythm was repeatedly interrupted by breaks for rain and bad light. Those breaks certainly affected his main bowling partner, fellow Surrey player Tony Lock, who sweated through 55 completely unproductive overs while Laker demolished the shell-shocked opposition.

There's every chance the Australians entered the game with a psychological disadvantage. In May, they'd collapsed against Surrey, when Laker took all 10 Australian scalps for only 88 runs.

ARRIVALS

Born this month:

5: James Lofton, NFL all-time receiver record (13,821 yds), with Green Bay Packers, LA Raiders, Buffalo Bills

9: Tom Hanks, US Academy Award-winning actor *(Philadelphia, Sleepless In Seattle, Forrest Gump)*

15: Ian Curtis, rock musician (Joy Division)

20: Charlie Magri, British world flyweight champion; Paul Cook, rock musician (Sex Pistols)

26: Dorothy Hamill, US figure-skating champion; Ramona Neubert, East German world record heptathlete and long jumper

30: Delta Burke, American TV actress

31: Michael Spink, former WBA light-heavyweight champion (1981), became IBF World heavyweight champ in 1985, retired in 1988 when beaten by Mike Tyson

JULY 26

Britian And France Rage As Nasser Grabs Suez Canal

FOUR YEARS TO THE DAY AFTER HE and a group of fellow army officers ousted King Farouk to begin creating a new republican Egypt, President Gamal Abdel Nasser outraged British and French leaders - but delighted his people - when he announced that he had nationalized the Anglo-French controlled Suez Canal Company.

In an emotion-charged speech to thousands of cheering supporters, Colonel Nasser switched from formal classical Arabic into Egyptian vernacular to tell imperialist powers that if they didn't like what he'd done, they could 'choke to death on their fury'.

Nasser's action is seen as retaliation to the recent refusal by Britain, the United States and the World Bank to finance the building of the Aswan High Dam - a project vital to the President's much-vaunted modernization plans. He'd been told that Egypt's economy was too fragile to support the project, but the Anglo-US decision was coloured by intelligence reports that Nasser had secretly purchased $200 million worth of arms from the Communist bloc, mortgaging Egyptian cotton crops for several years.

As Nasser spoke in the port of Alexandria, police were sealing the main entrance to the Canal Company's Cairo headquarters, cordoning off that building and the company's offices in Ismailia. While he has promised to pay compensation to shareholders and not to interfere with traffic on the French-built 103-mile waterway which links the Arabian Gulf oilfields and the Mediterranean, Britain and France are determined to take action.

During his speech, Colonel Nasser said he would use future Canal revenues to finance the Aswan project. The dam would, he said, increase Egypt's agricultural capacity by more than half and create huge amounts of hydro-electric power to help an industrialized Egypt 'compete with the West'.

The first public reaction to the announcement came from British Prime Minister, Sir Anthony Eden, who insisted that 'a man with Colonel Nasser's record cannot be allowed to have his thumb on our windpipe'.

Eden is especially concerned for the safety of Canal Company employees, many of whom are British. Nasser has threatened to imprison any who try to leave their jobs or flee Egypt, even though his shutdown of their offices makes it impossible for them to fulfil their contracts.

On July 28, Eden reinforced Britain's position when he ordered all Egyptian assets in Britain to be frozen and, two days later, imposed a total arms embargo on Egypt, telling Nasser he could not be allowed to have the Canal.

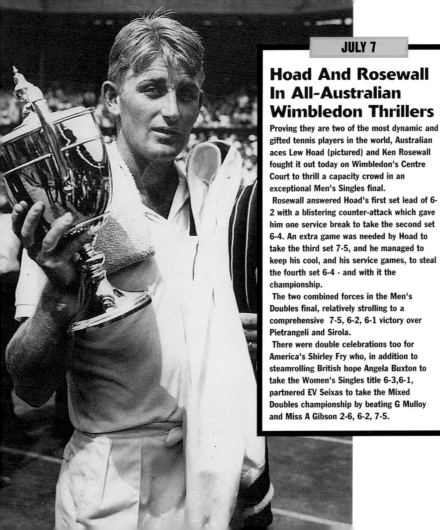

Hoad And Rosewall In All-Australian Wimbledon Thrillers

Proving they are two of the most dynamic and gifted tennis players in the world, Australian aces Lew Hoad (pictured) and Ken Rosewall fought it out today on Wimbledon's Centre Court to thrill a capacity crowd in an exceptional Men's Singles final.

Rosewall answered Hoad's first set lead of 6-2 with a blistering counter-attack which gave him one service break to take the second set 6-4. An extra game was needed by Hoad to take the third set 7-5, and he managed to keep his cool, and his service games, to steal the fourth set 6-4 - and with it the championship.

The two combined forces in the Men's Doubles final, relatively strolling to a comprehensive 7-5, 6-2, 6-1 victory over Pietrangeli and Sirola.

There were double celebrations too for America's Shirley Fry who, in addition to steamrolling British hope Angela Buxton to take the Women's Singles title 6-3,6-1, partnered EV Seixas to take the Mixed Doubles championship by beating G Mulloy and Miss A Gibson 2-6, 6-2, 7-5.

JULY

Suez Crisis: Conciliation Talks Begin – British And French Troops Sail

THE SUEZ CANAL CRISIS gained momentum this month as world governments tried to work out a plan acceptable to Egyptian President Nasser which would hand control of the strategic waterway to an international. Meanwhile, French and British troops began heading for the eastern Mediterranean, just in case force is needed to twist the Colonel's arm.

Events began unfolding on August 1 when British, French and US representatives began talks in London, calling the next day for international talks – an invitation Nasser rejected.

A 22-nation conference began on August 16, but not before British Prime Minister Sir Anthony Eden had made an official broadcast on August 8 when he told anxious Britons that force could not be ruled out if Nasser did not accept a 'reasonable' settlement.

After six days, the conference ended with a proposal was aimed at persuading Nasser to hand operational control of the Canal to an international board associated with the United Nations. Only four countries - the Soviet Union, India, Ceylon and Indonesia - refused to support the formula, but the 18 which did accounted for 95 per cent of the shipping which uses the Canal. On August 23 a five-nation team, including diplomats from the US, Ethiopia, Sweden and Iran, and led by Australian Prime Minister, Robert Menzies, left for Cairo.

Even as talks began, on August 28 Egypt expelled two British envoys, accusing them of spying. Two days later, the British government answered with the tit-for-tat expulsion of two Egyptian diplomats from London.

The build-up of French and British troops began early in the month when the aircraft carrier *HMS Theseus* left Portsmouth, carrying fighter aircraft and paratroops to Cyprus. Half of the 16th Parachute Brigade forces were said to be National Servicemen.

On August 29 it was announced in London that French troops were also to be based on Cyprus. Commanded by General André Beaufre, an airborne operations expert recalled from Algeria, the French began leaving the Mediterranean port of Marseilles in ships requisitioned by the Defense Ministry. While spokesmen in London and Paris continued to express official optimism at the prospects of a settlement agreement, the sheer weight of airborne manpower is a fair indication of planned strategy if talks fail.

Police And Army Vets May Run Meters

British motorists - especially those who live, drive and try to park in London - were underwhelmed today by a plan announced by Harold Watkinson, the Minister of Transport, which he believes could relieve the capital's increasing parking problems.

Taking his lead from the United States, where the idea seems to have worked well, the Minister intends to introduce parking meters onto London streets. They will, he suggests, be supervized by a new force of part-time traffic wardens.

Mr Watkinson suggests that ex-servicemen and policemen would make ideal recruits to the new workforce. While they would not have powers of arrest, he believes they could - in due course - help relieve the police of some traffic management duties. Revenues from the new meters could pay salaries, he says. The plan has received a 'cautious' welcome from Britain's two motoring organizations, The Automobile Association and The Royal Automobile Club, both of whom want to know more.

Sex Researcher Kinsey Asks Last Personal Question

Only sociologists would describe their mostly dry-as-a-bone, facts-and-figures science as 'sexy'. Alfred Kinsey, the American sociologist who died today at the age of 60, certainly did - especially when he turned his attention to the private habits of fellow Americans.

Professor Kinsey was a professor at Indiana University when he decided to interview 5,300 men about their sex lives, and the 1948 publication of his survey - entitled *The Sexual Behavior Of The Human Male* - created controversy and consternation, became the year's most unexpected best-seller and made a talk-show star out of its bemused author. Among Kinsey's findings, were the fact that 56 per cent of US men had been unfaithful to their wives, 90 per cent masturbated and 37 per cent had achieved orgasm with another man.

UK TOP 10 SINGLES

1: Whatever Will Be Will Be
- Doris Day

2: Why Do Fools Fall In Love
- Frankie Lymon & The Teenagers

3: Walk Hand In Hand
- Tony Martin

4: Sweet Old-Fashioned Girl
- Teresa Brewer

5: Mountain Greenery
- Mel Torme

6: Heartbreak Hotel
- Elvis Presley

7: I'll Be Home
- Pat Boone

8: Wayward Wind
- Tex Ritter

9: The Saints Rock 'n Roll
- Bill Haley & His Comets

10: Who Are We
- Ronnie Hilton

Music No Bar To Rock 'n' Roll Kids

While grown-ups fussed and fought over racial integration of southern schools and public transportation, America's teenagers developed a welcome colour blindness this summer as rock 'n' roll took a hold. Given it was a blend of black and white music forms, teenagers' decision to 'dig it' - regardless of whether the artist was Caucasian or negro - was a healthy and welcome sign of change which boded well for the future. The most remarkable display of the phenomenon came this month at the Maryland concert starring white hillbilly rocker Carl Perkins, R&B star Chuck Berry (pictured) and Frankie Lymon and The Teenagers, who'd just become the first black American act to top the British charts. More than 70,000 kids packed the completely integrated arena.

Car Crash Claims Action Painter Pollock

THE SUDDEN AND VIOLENT DEATH of American painter Jackson Pollock - killed outright today when his speeding car crashed into a tree near his Long Island home - was a fitting, if tragic, end to a life best remembered for the often violent and apparently random methods the 44 year old used to create his controversial 'action paintings' which divided the world's artistic community when he first produced them in 1947.

A native of Cody, Wyoming, Pollock became a student of Thomas Hart Benson at the Art Students' League, New York in the late 1920s. His increasingly abstract works in the early 1940s combined his interest in European surrealism and mystical imagery drawn from a period of Jungian psychoanalysis. But it was his action paintings which earned him immortality.

Pollock would pour and drip his colours on his large canvases (which were often laid out on the floor), working them with palette knives or sticks, and sometimes adding metallic paint, broken glass or sand to create what were, despite appearances, carefully created images and textures. The final composition would often be a section selected from the original canvas.

Much-imitated and often reviled by traditionalists, Pollock helped establish a new 'language' for art in the second half of this century.

Final Lines Drawn For US Election

It was convention time in San Francisco and Chicago this month as Republican and Democratic Party delegates met to spend a week doing whatever delegates do for a week before nominating their presidential and vice-presidential candidates with the traditional brouhaha and banner-waving.

The Republicans had a more relaxed time of it, naturally. With their President Eisenhower already in The White House and their Vice-President seeking unopposed re-nomination, they were able to party hard in San Francisco until August 22 when Ike and Nixon were given their triumphal dues.

By the time this happened, the GOP folk knew who the opposition were going to be in November. In the Democratic heartland of Mayor Richard Daley's Chicago, Adlai Stevenson was confirmed as their presidential candidate.

The next morning, Stevenson announced his choice of v-p running-mate. Rejecting the blandishments, promises and under-the-counter deals of front-runners John Kennedy and Hubert Humphrey, he nominated the duly-elected Senator Estes Kefauver.

Who? Quite. Which is why the Republican's Californian party was, by all accounts, a humdinger.

Lonnie's Smash Creates D-I-Y Music Boom

Amid all the hullabaloo surrounding the rock 'n' roll revolution, the arrival and astonishing success of Lonnie Donegan was, in its way, every bit as important as the rise of teenage idols. Very few could realistically aspire to being the next Elvis or Pat Boone. But just about anyone could tackle skiffle, which was what the style of music played by this 25 year old British guitarist-singer was called.

A folk and blues fan since his teens, Donegan - whose real name was Tony, but who'd taken the name Lonnie in tribute to his idol, American blues singer Lonnie Johnson - played banjo in jazz bands after doing his National Service.

It was while he was with the Ken Collyer Jazz Band that Donegan was given the chance to play so-called skiffle material, a raw blend of American folk and blues, and by 1951 he'd formed his own group. By 1953 he'd joined Chris Barber's Jazz Band, and it was in 1954 - during a Barber band session - that he filled in some spare time by recording *Rock Island Line,* a traditional song he'd characteristically modified, injecting it with sly humour.

Featured as a popular number in Barber concerts over the next 18 months, *Rock Island Line* was snapped up eagerly by record-buyers when some shrewd executive at Pye Records decided to release it as a single this January. An almost instant Top 10 hit, the record attracted the attention of Imperial Records in the US, becoming a million-seller soon after its release in March.

Besieged with tempting offers, Donegan quit the Barber band and began a hit-making career which should put him in pride of place in any book dealing with the major music influences of the fifties and early sixties - not least because

his success led to an explosion of amateur skiffle outfits who discovered you could just as easily create a double bass by threading cord through a hole in a tea chest, Mum's washboard and a couple of thimbles made a sound and rhythm almost like that of brushes on a snare drum, and the guy with the guitar only had to master three chords to give your 'band' access to the full folk and blues repertoire.

Donegan's track record over the next few years was remarkable. And if his chart record in the US put him pretty well in the One Hit Wonder class, in Britain he'd have huge success with songs like *Lost John, Stewball, Bring A Little Water Sylvie, Don't You Rock Me Daddy-O, Cumberland Gap, Gamblin' Man, Putting On The Style, Tom Dooley* and *My Dixie Darling,* most of them re-workings of traditional American songs.

Between 1954 and 1959, only Elvis Presley sold more singles in Britain than Lonnie Donegan, and his success inspired a number of other accomplished musicians to have a go at - and have hits with - this thing called skiffle.

TOMMY ROCKS IN CAVEMAN-STYLE

A desperate hunt by British record companies for a home-grown rock 'n' roll star appeared to be solved in October by the launch and immediate Top 20 status of Tommy Steele, a 19 year old Bermondsey - born cheerful cockney whose *Rock With The Caveman* sparked a marketing hype which remains unparalleled even to this day.

The campaign, and the young ex-deckhand's transformation from Tommy Hicks to the tougher-sounding Tommy Steele, was the work of Larry Parnes, who would go on to build a 'stable' of re-named British rockers. Thus, Reginald Smith became Marty Wilde, Ron Wycherley became Billy Fury, and the touring stages of Britain were soon paying host to the likes of Vince Eager, Georgie Fame, Duffy Power, Dickie Pride and Johnny Gentle. Spot a trend there?

Within three months The Tommy Steele Story was into production, and its youthful star was busy moving away from rock 'n' roll to begin a career with pop hits like *Singing The Blues, Handful Of Songs* and *Butterfingers* and turning into what he'd always said was his life's ambition - an all-round entertainer.

Making movies like *Tommy The Toreador* and *Half A Sixpence,* Steele became a gifted sculptor (his statue of Charlie Chaplin permanently graces London's Leicester Square, while his Eleanor Rigby watches over the old site of The Cavern Club in Liverpool), and turned into a song-and-dance man who still packs 'em into Britain's biggest theatres.

The Goons - wisely ended the joke before it was worn out

YOU WANT SILLY? CALL IN THE GOONS!

Comedy on record is very hard, if not impossible, to get right. It's all very well to act the fool in front of a microphone, but to make something which bears repeated listening - and is funny enough to make thousands of people spend their hard-earned cash and make it a hit - is an art in itself.

Peter Sellers, Spike Milligan and Harry Secombe knew how to make hit comedy. As The Goons, their surreal brand of lunacy had made them among Britain's biggest radio stars of the past three years. So when they decided to turn their attention to this new rock 'n' roll thing, the results were suitably bizarre, and hugely popular.

Releasing *I'm Walking Backwards For Christmas* in July was a master stroke. How many Christmas songs would they have as competition in the middle of summer? When airplay on the 'B' side, *Bluebottle Blues,* picked up, they had an instant Top 10 double-sided smash on their hands.

By September they'd rushed out an equally-successful sequel - *Bloodnock's Rock 'n' Roll Call,* teamed with the extremely strange *Ying Tong Song.* While Peter Sellers would tackle the pop business on his later solo albums and Harry Secombe would emerge as one of Britain's most popular near-operatic tenors, The Goons' flirtation with the charts wisely ended before the joke was worn out.

SEPT

Millions Tune In To See Elvis Make Sullivan Debut

A STAGGERING 82 PER CENT of America's potential 54 million TV viewers are reckoned to have turned on their sets tonight to catch the first Ed Sullivan Show appearance of Elvis Presley. Although the 21 year old teen sensation had already appeared on Milton Berle's Hollywood-based show and many regional programmes, his booking on America's top-rated and most influential variety showcase was widely known to have been made despite the misgivings of its stone-faced host.

Clearly bemused by the wave of screams and shrieks which almost drowned his introduction, the off-camera Sullivan was appalled by Presley's gyrations as he tore into his raucous new single Hound Dog.

If the relative calm of the ballad Love Me Tender - the theme song from Elvis' just-completed film debut which he also sang - mollified Sullivan a little, it did nothing to moderate his overall distaste for Elvis in particular, and rock 'n' roll in general. Aware that he would have to re-book this young superstar, Sullivan made it a condition of future appearances that Elvis would only be seen from the waist up!

The TV debut of Love Me Tender created an historical precedent all its own. Audience reaction was so positive, more than a million American teens placed orders for the still unrecorded song with local record stores. It became the first single to qualify for a Gold Disk before it went on sale.

President Eisenhower Demands Integration Speed-Up

Tired of the slow rate of progress in many southern states, and confronted with the state of emergency declared three days ago to subdue growing violence against blacks attempting to attend schools in Clinton, Tennessee, President Eisenhower today stepped into the front line of the integration debate. He demanded that all states conform to the Supreme Court ruling which called for an end to segregated education in all publicly-funded schools and colleges, and the protection of black students attending them.

Under the terms of the constitution, the President's authority is limited to federal affairs, so each of the states involved can continue to stonewall full compliance, or continue to make the transformation piecemeal.

But his public and vehement statement is clear warning to segregationists that they are swimming against a mounting tide they'd be foolish to ignore - especially as Ike is in a position to withdraw or slow down federal grants many states could not survive without.

Haley Rock Film Sparks Teddy Boy Riots

British civic leaders and police chiefs faced a unique challenge this month when screenings of *Rock Around The Clock,* the first rock 'n' roll movie, triggered riots by dancing, cheering Teddy Boys - youths who adopt a distinctive dress code of long Edwardian style jackets, tight 'drainpipe' trousers and slicked-back pompadour hair styles with long sideburns.

Up and down the country police were called in to cinemas where the film - starring rock 'n' roll pioneer Bill Haley in a teens v oldies story made in only two weeks with a budget of $450,000 - was showing. In some cases, seats were wrenched from their floor fixtures and fireworks were let off, but in others the disturbances were restricted to widespread

outbreaks of jive-dancing in the aisles.

As magistrates courts began to fill with teenagers facing charges of insulting behaviour and vandalism, a number of towns' Watch Committees either pulled the movie off local screens, or outlawed its intended showing. Just like the fictional wrinklies in *Rock Around The Clock* reacted, in fact!

44

SEPTEMBER 28
Japan And USSR Agree Truce Formula

Unbelievably, eleven years after the rest of the world signed the many deals and treaties which ended World War II, Japan and the USSR are still officially at war with each other and still carry out their diplomatic discussions via third-parties.

That state of affairs - created by the late Josef Stalin's refusal to deal with the Japanese while they had unresolved territorial disputes left over from before the war and US naval and air bases were sited on Japanese soil - could finally be over soon.

Today, in Moscow, the two nations announced that they had agreed a formula which should end their state of war, beginning with a restoration of diplomatic relations.

SEPTEMBER 18
Gold Coast Independence

In the midst of worldwide and often-bloody confrontations with colonies seeking independence and self-determination - including Kenya, Cyprus, Malaya, Singapore - the British government today revealed the date on which The Gold Coast will become Britain's first independent black African colony. History will be made on March 6, 1957 when the Union Jack will be lowered from flagpoles.

SEPTEMBER 29
Britain And France To Take Suez Row To UN

A month of stalemate between Britain, France, the US, 18 other nations and the Egyptian government of President Nasser came to a head today with the announcement in Paris that an Anglo-French coalition is to take the Suez Canal dispute to the United Nations Security Council.

Having initially said that he would accept any solution which did not affect Egyptian sovereignty, on September 9 Nasser flatly rejected last month's US plan for international management of the Canal, and did the same when Secretary of State Dulles drew up a new one which a second 18-nation Suez Canal Conference in London ratified on September 21, along with the founding of a Canal Users' Association.

Nasser's rejection was undoubtedly coloured by the decision of the Anglo-French Suez Canal Company to allow its 160 non-Egyptian pilots to walk out on their jobs, leaving the Egyptians with only 65 staff to handle shipping movements.

British Prime Minister Sir Anthony Eden arrived in Paris this morning with Foreign Secretary Selwyn Lloyd for crisis talks with French premier Guy Mollet and his Foreign Minister, Christian Pineau, at which the decision was taken to go to the UN. While their communiqué said Anglo-French solidarity had been strengthened 'in every respect', observers noted that references to 'further studies' being needed to remove 'minor points outstanding' between the two nations suggests the press announcement hid more than it disclosed.

Cyprus Toffee-Tin Bomb Blast Injures Soldiers

A BIZARRE AND DEADLY twist in the continuing struggle in Cyprus today when seven British soldiers were injured - three of them critically - in a military base rest room by a bomb hidden in an apparently-innocent toffee tin.

The bombing followed the previous day's fatal shooting of a British army doctor driving through Nicosia and came as the seven - recently arrived in Cyprus - were about to hear an acclimatization lecture which would have included advice on bomb attacks and the need for extreme vigilance.

As ambulance men fought their way through dust, fumes and wreckage to rescue the men, hundreds of civilian employees were being rounded up for questioning by military police.

Also being questioned are the three EOKA men who were discovered burying a glass jar by a Royal Horse Guards mountain patrol. It is said to contain a 250,000-word 'war diary', allegedly notes written by EOKA leader George Grivas.

If genuine, the document would link Grivas and the exiled Archbishop Makarios in a murderous conspiracy plot.

Haley Rocks On With Five UK Smashes

Bill Haley continued to maintain his dominance over Elvis Presley in the British charts this month - scoring no less than five Top 20 hits simultaneously to establish a permanent place in the record books. While Presley's new single *Hound Dog* roared in and lodged at No. 3 in the *New Musical Express* chart for eight weeks, Bill Haley and The Comets sailed through October with *Rockin' Through The Rye* (at No. 6), a re-released *Rock Around The Clock* (at 10), *The Saints Rock 'n' Roll* (13), *Razzle Dazzle* (a new entry at No. 16) and the teen catch-phrase creator *See You Later Alligator* (also newly-entered at No. 17). Back in the US, a deliriously-happy Columbia Pictures were busy shooting a rush-release sequel to their incredible money-maker. It is to be titled *Don't Knock The Rock.* This time, producer Sam Katzman has an increased budget of $600,000 to play with, but still has a two-week shooting deadline to meet.

Suez Zone Explodes: Israel Invades Gaza, Britain Bombs Cairo

AS DUSK FELL ON EGYPT this evening, waves of RAF Vickers Valiant and Canberra bombers began to hit military targets near Cairo and the Canal Zone city of Port Said. The official British line is that the attacks were launched to ensure the Canal remained open to international traffic, an objective jeopardized by an Israeli invasion of the Gaza Strip and the Sinai Peninsula two days ago.

There are doubts about this version of events, with the United States furious and bitter that Britain and France kept them in the dark, and suggesting complicity with Israel. That anger intensified at an emergency session of the UN Security Council tonight when the French vetoed a US resolution calling for 'all UN members to refrain from the use of force, or the threat of force and to refrain from giving aid to Israel' - an obvious reference to Britain and France. The Soviet Union supported the resolution.

Inevitably, the background is complex, but the Israeli's surprise invasion - with heavily-armoured forces driving unopposed to within 20 miles of the Canal - was said to be a retaliation for Egyptian attacks on Israeli land and sea communications. The Israelis had mobilized in secret, and only attacked once they had 400,000 reservists to support their 30,000 invasion force.

It is known that President Eisenhower twice contacted Israel's Prime Minister, David Ben-Gurion, asking him not to endanger the fragile peace, and that the State Department ordered the evacuation of all US citizens from Israel and Egypt shortly before the invasion. Which means the US knew something, if not everything.

In London, Sir Anthony Eden was said to have followed the US lead by asking Israel to lay off. Logic suggests that, if the UK really was neutral in the matter, British bombers should have hit Israeli positions too, and not confined themselves to decimating the Egyptians' ability to respond.

Eden's reasoning is that while Israel responded to an Anglo-French ultimatum for a cessation of hostilities by saying it would pull back if the Egyptians did likewise, President Nasser had refused, describing it as 'an attack on the rights and dignity of Egypt'.

It is also known that, even as the bombers flew in from Cyprus, a huge British amphibious force with an escort of warships had left Valetta harbour in Malta and was headed east, towards the Egyptian coast.

Only one thing is clear: Britain and France now stand isolated from the world community, with the rare sight of American and Soviet UN delegates voting together as proof. Meanwhile, Egypt is being smashed from the air, has been over-run on its land front, and seems about to be hit from the sea.

UK TOP 10 SINGLES

1: A Woman In Love
- Frankie Laine

2: Lay Down Your Arms
- Anne Shelton

3: Hound Dog
- Elvis Presley

4: Whatever Will Be Will Be
- Doris Day

5: Giddy-Up-A-Ding-Dong
- Freddie Bell & The Bellboys

6: Rockin' Through The Rye
- Bill Haley & His Comets

7: The Great Pretender/Only You
- The Platters

8: Bloodnock's Rock 'n' Roll Call/Ying Tong Song
- The Goons

9: Bring A Little Water Sylvie/Dead Or Alive
- Lonnie Donegan

10: Rock Around The Clock
- Bill Haley & His Comets

Khrushchev Wrong-Footed As Poles, Hungarians Rise In Revolt

HARDLINE OPPONENTS OF Soviet leader Nikita Khrushchev's relatively 'soft' approach towards the USSR's European satellites, and who have serious misgivings at his apparent willingness to let loyal puppet regime masters be ousted by more liberal politicians, had reason to feel smug this month as two leading Warsaw Pact countries - Poland and Hungary - were wracked by anti-Russian riots.

Within days events in both countries were at crisis point. On October 20, Khrushchev was forced to take the unimaginable (in Stalin's day) and demeaning (in hardliners' eyes) step of flying to Poland in person to tell the new government of Wladyslaw Gomulka - released from prison by Khrushchev in April - they were moving too fast towards their stated objective of independence from the USSR and a separate Polish road to socialism. Khrushchev left Gomulka in no doubt what Russia's response would be if the Poles continued to defy Moscow. But Gomulka refused Khrushchev's demand that Marshal Rokossovski - Russian-born but now claiming Polish citizenship - retain his place on the Polish Politburo. He will remain Defence Minister, however.

Even as the Soviet delegation returned to Moscow on October 25, the streets of Warsaw were filled with thousands of Poles renewing their call for an end to Russian domination, and voicing their support for Hungarians who are also trying to go their own way. There were clashes outside the Hungarian Embassy as rioters met police and truncheon-wielding Communist Party workers.

In Hungary itself, calls for reform, liberalization and release from Soviet control were not met with the same conciliatory tone. Three days of battles between Hungarian rebels, tank-supported Soviet troops and Hungary's dreaded secret police, the AVH, were believed to have left 3,000 people dead by October 26. Some Hungarian troops had joined the rebels.

The picture was confusing. People arriving at the Austrian border region said the capital, Budapest, was mostly in Hungarian hands, with rebels riding atop Russian tanks driven by troops who said they had no intention of firing on rebels. However, at least one person reported having seen a Russian tank fire into a crowd.

Fighting has been so heavy, Budapest looks as smashed as it did in 1945 when the Soviets first seized control. Many buildings bear the scars of tank cannon-fire and streets are littered with the wreckage of tram cars which the rebels used as barricades.

Imre Hagy, the new 'Titoist' prime minister, broadcast a pledge to begin negotiations for a withdrawal of all Soviet troops based in Hungary, but said he could not start until the armed revolt was ended. He also promised that democratization would be carried out 'without delay'.

That promise - which envisages a new system based on the superiority of the Communist Party, but will permit parliamentary representation by other parties - is bound to bring him into conflict with Moscow. Already there are ominous reports of five Soviet divisions being brought up to the East German-Hungarian border, with armoured forces on the move from Russia.

OCT

MAY 17
'SUGAR' RAY LEONARD - THE ULTIMATE CHAMPION

One of the greatest boxers of all time, 'Sugar' Ray Leonard was born today in Wilmington, North Carolina, to parents who named him after their hero, the blues-jazz singer Ray Charles. When their son proved his ring talents at the age of 14, it was inevitable that someone would tag the 'Sugar' prefix in tribute to another boxing great, and a musical career would be out of the question.

Leonard had a meteoric amateur career which climaxed with a light-welterweight gold medal in the 1976 Olympic Games in Montreal, after which he turned pro to help pay family bills - something he achieved by winning his first 27 fights and taking the world welterweight title in 1979, when he stopped Wilfred Benitez in the 15th round.

Beaten in an epic battle with Panamanian Roberto Duran in 1980 after successfully defending his title against Britain's Dave 'Boy' Green, he won the championship back later the same year when Duran controversially gave up in the eighth round.

Stepping up to light-middleweight in 1981, Leonard won the WBA version of that title in the same year, beating the formidable Thomas 'Hit Man' Hearns to emerge as undisputed world champ, but was forced into retirement after an operation to repair a detached retina.

Leonard returned to boxing a year later, retired again, and came back after three years to take the world middleweight title from Marvin Hagler in 1987 before taking the world light-heavyweight and super-middleweight titles, drawing with Hearns and beating Duran, the only boxer ever to have beaten him.

The first person to win world titles at five different

'Sugar' Ray Leonard

weights, Leonard has proved as agile in the business world as he was in the ring.

JANUARY 23
CLOSING CREDITS FOR KORDA, MOVIE MAKER SUPREME

One of the most remarkable success stories in the history of European film-making came to an end today with the death of Sir Alexander Korda, the Hungarian-born producer and director who saved, revived and transformed the British industry almost singlehanded in the thirties.

Korda, who was 67, came to London in 1931 and formed London Films - a production company which began its impressive run of international successes with the Charles Laughton extravaganza *The Private Lives Of Henry VIII*. A charming and witty man in six languages, Korda built his own production center at Denham Studios, from where he produced such films as *The Scarlet Pimpernel, Sanders Of The River,* the HG Wells sci-fi classic *Things To Come, The Ghost Goes West, Elephant Boy* and *The Four Feathers* before moving to Hollywood in 1940.

His five-year stay there resulted in *The Thief of Baghdad* and *Jungle Book,* among others, while his return to England saw him produce such hits as *The Fallen Idol, The Third Man,* the John Mills vehicle *Hobson's Choice* and Laurence Olivier's stunning *Richard III.*

JANUARY 18
AA MILNE - THE PARENT'S FRIEND

For close on 70 years, frazzled parents confronted by 'Read me a story!' demands from not-ready-to-sleep offspring have had reason to offer a silent thank-you to Alan Alexander Milne, who died today. The wonderful series of stories he wrote for his son in the 1920s and 30s remain a valuable source of bed-time pacification, never having been out of print in all that time.

Although his hero was fairly stupid, greedy and prone to pomposity, Milne created a timeless world for Winnie-the-Pooh, a bear of little brain. Along with a regular cast of characters like the ever-nervous Piglet, the doleful donkey Eeyore, the irrepressible bouncing Tigger, the not-as-smart-as-he-thought-he-was Owl, the maternal Kanga (not forgetting her baby, Roo) and the very sensible and

organized Rabbit, Pooh roamed The Hundred Acre Wood, a place the outside world never touched.

Based on stories he made up for his son, who really was called Christopher Robin and was naturally given a role to play in the gentle adventures Milne then committed to paper with such success, the story books - *Winnie-The-Pooh, The House At Pooh Corner* - and collections of verse - *When We Were Very Young* and *Now We Are Six* - were blessed by the addition of charming illustrations by EH Shepard. First published in 1928, *The House At Pooh Corner* made AA Milne a wealthy man. It also made bed-times less frazzled for countless thousands of others.

AUGUST 11
BERTOLT BRECHT - THE PEOPLE'S PLAYWRIGHT

Born in Bavaria, Brecht first became a success in 1928 when *The Threepenny Opera,* his re-working - with long-time friend and musical collaborator Kurt Weill - of John Gay's 18th century *The Beggar's Opera,* was a huge hit.

The rise of Hitler forced the strongly left-wing (though never communist, he swore) Brecht to emigrate to the United States. While living in Los Angeles, Brecht completed a number of landmark plays marked for their repeated exploration of the triumph of good over evil, of Everyman (or Woman) against repression - *The Good Woman Of Sechuan, Mother Courage* and *The Caucasian Chalk Circle.*

Driven from the US by accusations that he was a communist, Brecht returned to work in East Berlin where he continued to develop his radical theories of theatrical presentation, the worldwide impact of which cannot be overstated.

NOV

Victorious Ike Forces Suez Pull-Out By Shamed Eden

HIS HAND IMMEASURABLY STRENGTHENED by an overwhelming election victory over Democrat challenger Adlai Stevenson on November 6 - with an increased majority, despite Stevenson's last-minute attempt to question his health and raise the spectre of a replacement President Richard Nixon - President Eisenhower succeeded in forcing an embattled British premier Sir Anthony Eden to withdraw British troops from Egypt and hand control of the Suez Canal to an interim UN force.

The disastrous Anglo-French invasion of Egypt was a brutal two-day fiasco which began on November 5 with British amphibious and helicopter-borne marine commandos battling their way through Port Said while French forces over-ran Port Faud before heading south.

A paratroop assault on the Gamel military airfield near Port Said was met with resistance from Egyptian defenders armed with Russian tanks and 100mm self-propelled guns, but an air strike by RAF jet fighters helped achieve a speedy victory which was followed by an offer of surrender by Port Said's Egyptian governor - a surrender accepted by Brigadier MAH Butler, commander of the 16th Parachute Brigade, but withdrawn the next morning when Cairo ordered the governor to fight on.

Allied warships began bombarding Port Said, setting fire to the Shell oil refinery and forcing Egyptian tanks to retreat south while ground forces began a street-by-street takeover of the town. Allied casualties were light, with 30 paratroops injured during landings. There were a reported 70 Egyptian fatalities.

By midnight on November 8, the Anglo-French expedition had succeeded in destroying 95 per cent of the Egyptian air force, but had not gained total control of the Canal Zone. That was denied them by universal condemnation in the United Nations, where an immediate-withdrawal resolution was passed, and a flurry of bellicose threats came from Soviet leader Marshal Bulganin.

Behind the scenes, President Eisenhower and Secretary of State John Foster Dulles - both livid with Britain and France, and still refusing to believe they hadn't colluded with Israel - went for Eden's jugular. As the pound plummeted on world money markets, the US Treasury told Chancellor of the Exchequer Harold Macmillan that American support for sterling depended entirely on a British pull-out from Egypt.

Attacked by political opponents in parliament, press, radio, TV and huge public demonstrations, and abandoned by once-loyal colleagues, Eden was a defeated and shamed man. On November 19 a communiqué from 10 Downing Street announced he was suffering from 'severe overstrain' and would - on his doctors' advice - be flying to Jamaica for a three-week break. In his absence, temporary charge of the cabinet would be taken by RAB Butler, Leader of The House of Commons.

On November 21, Britain's disgrace was completed when the first of an eventual 1,000-strong UN force arrived in Port Said to begin taking over management of the Canal from remaining Anglo-French troops.

NOVEMBER 30

Student Leader Castro Attacks Cuban Police Station

The authority of Cuban leader Fulgencio Batista was threatened today by a series of armed raids on rural police stations by insurgents led by Fidel Castro (pictured) a one-time student dissident jailed by Batista but now returned from exile in Mexico. Batista, whose corrupt regime is amply funded by a thriving gambling and prostitution-led tourist industry, its world-famous tobacco products, thriving sugar plantations and the unconditional support of successive American governments, says he will crush Castro, whose stated objective is the formation of a socialist state on the island republic.

Born this month:
4: Joan Rodgers, classical soprano
6: Graeme Wood, Australian Test cricketer
11: Ian Craig Marsh, pop musician (Human League)
23: Shane Gould, Australian world champion freestyle swimmer, Olympic Gold medal winner 1972 (200 metres individual medley)
28: Lucy Gutteridge, UK actress

DEPARTURES

Died this month:
4: Art Tatum, seminal and hugely-influential US jazz pianist-composer, soloist, group leader and accompanist
26: Tommy Dorsey (Thomas Francis Dorsey), US big band leader, trombonist, composer

NOVEMBER 1

Ernie Gets Ready As Bonds Go On Sale

The British - as Britons do - began their involvement in the start of new national savings scheme which gives owners of the new £1 ($3) Premium Bonds a monthly chance to win up to £1,000 tax-free   by forming long neat lines outside the hundreds of post offices which are selling them.

 No reported fights. No fuss. Just a steady procession of punters which created a first-day fund of £2 million ($6m) for the government to play with.

 In Blackpool, where staff have the responsibility of feeding Bond numbers into ERNIE (Electronic Random Number Indicator Equipment), the giant computer which will randomly pick each month's lucky numbers, the scene was described as 'complete chaos'. Remember, this was in the days before personal computers, so numbers had to be keyed in manually!

Soviets Send In Tanks To Crush Hungarian Revolution

THE HUNGARIAN REVOLUTION IS OVER, crushed beneath the tracks of an estimated 1,000 Red Army tanks which today ploughed through the streets of Budapest while aircraft, artillery and infantry smashed the ill-armed Hungarian resistance into submission. Despite attempts by Soviet troops to seal off Hungarian-Austrian border, thousands have begun escaping to the West.

City centre fighting was concentrated on the Defence Ministry and Parliament, both of which fell within hours. There was confusion about the fate of Prime Minister Imre Nagy, last heard during a 5.15 am broadcast when he told Radio Budapest listeners of the Russian attack. The station itself went off the air at 8.10 as a lone voice appealed for Western aid: 'Help Hungary!...Help!...Help!'

There's reason to believe that the Soviets decided definitely to act on November 2 when Nagy told Moscow's ambassador, Yuri Andropov, that Hungary intended to quit the Warsaw Pact and become a neutral state - an unacceptable proposition.

A dramatic first-hand account of fighting reached the West in messages sent via teleprinter by a reporter at the *Szabad Nep* newspaper. Breaking off transmissions to fire at Russians from his window, he described tram barricades, young people making Molotov cocktails and grenades to hurl at the tanks.

'What is the United Nations doing?' he typed. 'Give us a little encouragement. We will hold out to our last drop of blood'. At 10.55 am, the line was cut.

Soviet duplicity was characterized by the arrest of General Pal Maleter, the Hungarian military commander, while he was in talks to arrange the withdrawal of Russian troops from Hungary - talks called by Moscow to cover their preparations for invasion.

There's Hungarian duplicity, too. The lunchtime news bulletin from Moscow Radio announced that the Hungarian counter-revolution had been crushed and the formation of a 'Revolutionary Workers and Peasants Government' was to be headed by Janos Kadar, a man who'd claimed to support Nagy's liberalization programme.

Confronted by international horror at the brutality of their invasion - typified by a November 9 UN resolution calling for a withdrawal of their troops, a condemnatory message from President Eisenhower to Bulganin and wholesale resignations from national Communist parties worldwide - the Soviets replied by commencing an even-tougher persecution of those Hungarians known to have created or supported their country's bid for freedom.

They would continue to meet brave resistance in the coming months, but Moscow had sent a clear message to all its satellites: the USSR's steel gauntlet contained an iron fist.

Soviets Apply Martial Law Clamp On Hungary

THE SOVIET UNION BEGAN to squeeze the last remaining pockets of Hungarian resistance to their invasion and the authority of the puppet government led by turncoat Prime Minister Janos Kadar when a state of martial law was declared by President Dobi this evening.

The move - which means occupying Red Army forces have *carte blanche* to turn their guns on dissidents - came in response to a 24-hour strike call from the Budapest Workers' Council as protest against the Kadar regime.

The decree Dobi signed to formalize martial law establishes 'instant justice' courts to try people accused of inciting revolt (a catch-all charge which stamps out free speech and eliminates criticism of any kind), jeopardizing production (which means no strikes for any reason), the illegal possession of arms, murder and looting.

The last-named offence probably doesn't include Communist Party officials who've busied themselves 'confiscating' the homes and possessions of arrested dissidents and those who've fled to the West. And murder will not be attached to the systematic elimination, after show trials, of those who led the bid to gain Hungarian freedom.

According to the decree, these measures had been made necessary 'owing to the continued activities of counter-revolutionary elements'.

Stardom For Sex-Kitten Bardot

Forget Monroe - the international big-screen sex symbol of 1956 is sultry French actress Brigitte Bardot. Aged 22, her smouldering performance in the steamy drama *And God Created Woman* (pictured) has had male movie critics and film buffs lost for words and short of breath, and caused the usual bunch of killjoys to try have it pulled from British and American screens.

Directed by her lover Roger Vadim, who is said to have discovered Bardot when she was a 17 year old aspiring model, *And God Created Woman* showed an awful lot of BB's remarkably attractive charms and probably quadrupled holiday bookings to its French Riviera location. It also led to an invitation for her to appear with British heart-throb Dirk Bogarde in the comedy *Doctor At Sea,* filmed in England with a horde of press photographers lurking round every corner.

Selected as this year's Royal Command Film, the annual charity gala evening the film industry throws, *Doctor At Sea* gave the Queen a chance to see what the headlines were all about when Bardot appeared near-nude in a shower scene.

DECEMBER 2

Batista Claim: Castro Is Dead

Cuban hard-man Fulgencio Batista today claimed that Fidel Castro - the 30 year old rebel leader has been killed in a Cuban Air Force raid in Oriente province. If the news is true, and no positive proof has yet been offered to confirm Batista's statement, Castro's death marks the end of a remarkable adventure which began on July 26, 1953. That was the day that the former student, son of a wealthy middle-class family, launched a suicidal frontal attack on an army post in the town of Moncada which left 100 soldiers dead. After fleeing to Mexico, where he was taught his warfare crafts, Castro returned to Cuba last year with an initial 80 supporters, to begin harrassing government outposts and recruiting peasant militia.

DECEMBER 14

Eden Returns To Face The Cost Of Defeat

SIR ANTHONY EDEN RETURNED to London today from his enforced Jamaican rest cure, refreshed enough to begin facing the real cost of his disastrous misreading and mishandling of the Suez crisis, but clearly not fully recovered from the strain which had made his doctors insist he take a break.

It is an open secret that the Prime Minister had not been 100 percent fit for some time. In 1953 he'd had three major operations to remove an obstruction in his bile duct, though the bile his actions have attracted from Britain's once-staunch allies - especially an openly-hostile President Eisenhower - has obviously taken its toll on his energy and confidence.

While he was away, the stand-in government leader RAB Butler had been forced to order the withdrawal of British troops still on the Egyptian front-line, go cap in hand to US and Canadian treasury chiefs asking them to waive loan interest due this month and arrange to borrow a staggering $1,300 million from the International Monetary Fund.

Eden's rash adventure - and its aftermath - had effectively bankrupted Britain. No-one believes he will be able to remain in office for much longer. He would, in fact, announce his resignation and retirement from politics on January 9, handing over to Harold Macmillan, whose task it would be to begin repairing Anglo-US relations.

DECEMBER 20

Israel Digs Into Gaza As Canal Clean-Up Starts

No-one believed the Suez crisis would be ended simply by forcing Britain and France to pull their forces out of Egypt. There's still the question of Israel, the country whose capture of disputed border territories supposedly forced the Anglo-French team into action.

Last month's announcement by Foreign Minister Golda Meir that Israel intended staying in the Gaza Strip region which runs along the coast between Egypt and Israel, was greeted with alarm, and the international community has spent the intervening weeks trying to persuade Israel to quit the area.

They got their answer today in Tel Aviv when a government spokesman confirmed Israel's determination to hang on to Gaza, regardless of the sanctions threats which have been made.

One ray of hope came on December 28 when an international team of UN-backed divers began work on removing the first of a number of ships ordered to be sunk in the Canal to block traffic. It will be a long process, but it's hoped that the strategic link will be usable again, saving world container ships a costly detour around the African coastline.

Has Rock Killed The Christmas Spirit?

Time was, at this time of the year the tills in record shops would be ringing a merry melody as people suspended their good sense and rushed to buy some sentimental or cute nonsense celebrating the holiday season. This year there seems to be no demand for vinyl Yuletide greetings - and some are saying rock 'n' roll has made the Christmas hit a thing of the past.

A look at the US and British charts confirms the theory. Where, in previous years, you'd catch sight of a red-nosed reindeer or Mommy kissin' (oh, horror!) Santa Claus, and swear you could hear sleighbells ringing across snow-covered vistas, a very different picture emerges.

Britain's No. 1 this month - as it was last month and would remain into January - was the heart-wrenching Johnnie Ray opus *Just Walkin' In The Rain.* Not snow, you'll note. In America, the top spot was hardly any cheerier. Guy Mitchell was lodged there, determinedly telling whoever cared to listen that he never felt more like *Singing The Blues.*

The only snuggle-up songs came from Elvis Presley *(Love Me Tender and Love Me)* and the High Society movie teaming of Bing Crosby and Grace Kelly, whose *True Love* was melting hearts on both sides of the Atlantic.

YOUR 1956 HOROSCOPE

Unlike most Western horoscope systems which group astrological signs into month-long periods based on the influence of 12 constellations, the Chinese believe that those born in the same year of their calendar share common qualities, traits and weaknesses with one of 12 animals - Rat, Ox, Tiger, Rabbit, Dragon, Snake, Horse, Sheep, Monkey, Rooster, Dog or Pig.

They also allocate the general attributes of five natural elements - Earth, Fire, Metal, Water, Wood - and an overall positive or negative aspect to each sign to summarize its qualities.

If you were born between January 24, 1955 and February 11, 1956, you are a Sheep. As this book is devoted to the events of 1956, let's take a look at the sign which governs those born between February 12 that year and January 30, 1957 - The Year of The Monkey:

THE MONKEY
FEBRUARY 12, 1956 - JANUARY 30, 1957
ELEMENT: FIRE ASPECT: +

Monkeys display cleverness, intelligence and quick wits and can size up any situation at a glance. With a natural cunning which gives them an ingenious and inventive mind, Monkeys learn the intricacies of social skills - how to mingle, learn and take from other people, and how to get exactly what they want from a relationship - from an early age. Their poise and self-assurance never runs out as it comes from vast resources of inborn charm which ensures them general popularity and also guarantees them fulfilment of their aims and ambitions.

Monkeys are so inventive they tend to confuse fantasy with reality so, in their scheme of things, truth and untruth often make easy bedfellows. If they are caught out, Monkeys will always somehow manage to twist the situation to their advantage to vindicate themselves and save face.

Rarely bored, Monkeys are extremely inquisitive and forever seeking the bigger and better they need to keep themselves interested and amused. Mischievous and impish, Monkeys are always trying to liven things up.

Some Monkeys can manipulate others too easily. They can read people like books and female Monkeys can play rather subtle games with those of the opposite sex, seducing them with their feminine charms.

Highly adaptable and versatile, Monkeys pick up new skills and techniques in the blink of an eye - a tremendous asset for them in all areas of life and work. With such an agile mentality, problem-solving is both their forte and their joy. They have the ability to turn their hands to anything which will bring them ultimate success and, in many cases, make their fortune.

Though their renowned adaptability takes them into many occupations, Monkeys naturally go for show business because they have a compelling need to be noticed and leave a memory of themselves behind. However, they don't really care about their reputations, so it doesn't matter to them if the impression they create is one of pleasure or shock - it's simply a case of the bigger the publicity, the happier they are.

FAMOUS MONKEYS

Sebastian Coe
British Olympic and world champion athlete, politician

Elizabeth Taylor
Oscar-winning actress, multiple matrimonialist

Walter Matthau
Oscar-winning actor

Diana Ross
singing superstar, actress

Pope John Paul II

Tim Rice
lyricist, author

Sugar Ray Leonard
former world welterweight boxing champion

Martina Navratilova
tennis supremo

Nigel Kennedy
eccentric violin virtuoso